SKOKIE PUBLIC LIBRARY

3 1232 00823 2318

D1292935

Hauling a Pumpkin

Wheels and Axles vs. Lever

by Mari Schuh

first step nonfiction

Lerner Publications ◆ Minneapolis

LERNER

SOURCE

Expand learning beyond the printed book. Download free, complementary educational resources for this book from our website, www.lerneresource.com.

Copyright © 2016 by Lerner Publishing Group, Inc.

All rights reserved. International copyright secured. No part of this book may be reproduced, stored in a retrieval system, or transmitted in any form or by any means—electronic, mechanical, photocopying, recording, or otherwise—without the prior written permission of Lerner Publishing Group, Inc., except for the inclusion of brief quotations in an acknowledged review.

All images in this book are used with the permission of: © Todd Strand/Independent Picture Service except: © HomeArt/Shutterstock.com, p. 8 (bottom); © iStockphoto.com/DonNichols, p. 8 (top left); © iStockphoto.com/venturecx, p. 8 (top right).
Front cover: © Todd Strand/Independent Picture Service.

Main body text set in ITC Avant Garde Gothic Std Medium 21/25.
Typeface provided by Adobe Systems.

Lerner Publications Company
A division of Lerner Publishing Group, Inc.
241 First Avenue North
Minneapolis, MN 55401 USA

For reading levels and more information, look up this title at www.lernerbooks.com.

Library of Congress Cataloging-in-Publication Data

Cataloging-in-Publication Data for *Hauling a Pumpkin: Wheels and Axels vs. Levers* is on file at the Library of Congress.
ISBN: 978-1-4677-8026-1 (LB)
ISBN: 978-1-4677-8304-0 (PB)
ISBN: 978-1-4677-8305-7 (EB)

Manufactured in the United States of America
1 – CG – 7/15/15

Table of Contents

Noah wants to bring home a pumpkin.

The pumpkin is heavy! What can help him carry it?

Noah's mom spots a shovel.
The handle is a **lever**. She
6 thinks it might help Noah.

Noah wishes he had his wagon. Wagons have **wheels and axles** to move things.

lever

wheel

axle

A lever and wheels and axles are types of **simple machines**.

Noah pushes the pumpkin onto the shovel.

The handle is the **arm** of
the lever.

A lever has an arm and a fulcrum.

The arm turns on a **fulcrum**.

One end of the arm goes
down. One end goes up.

A lever stays
in one place.

Noah's mom lifts the
pumpkin. But she can't
move it.

Noah Tries Wheels and Axles

Then Noah sees a wagon!

A wagon's wheels and axles might get the job done.

The wagon has four wheels.

Axles connect the wheels.

Wheels and axles turn.
When the wheels turn, the
axles turn too.

Noah's mom lifts the pumpkin into the wagon.

Noah Moves the Pumpkin

Noah pulls the wagon.

He can move the pumpkin!

Wheels and axles help things move.

How can you use wheels and axles?

Glossary

arm – the part of a lever that rests and moves on a fixed point

fulcrum – the point on which a lever's bar rests and turns

lever – a bar that lifts or lowers objects on a fixed point

simple machines – machines with one moving part or no moving parts

wheels and axles – wheels and rods that move together

Index